A Tilt

To Keith, on his
birthday.

— Rupa

A Tilt

poems

Farideh de Bosset

Inanna Poetry & Fiction Series

Inanna Publications and Education Inc.
Toronto, Canada

Canada Council for the Arts **Conseil des Arts du Canada** 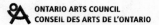 **ONTARIO ARTS COUNCIL** **CONSEIL DES ARTS DE L'ONTARIO**

The publisher gratefully acknowledges the support of the Canada Council for the Arts and the Ontario Arts Council for its publishing program.

The publisher is also grateful for the kind support received from an Anonymous Fund at The Calgary Foundation.

Cover artwork: Elizabeth Macdonald, "Blue Moon"

Cover/interior design by Luciana Ricciutelli

Library and Archives Canada Cataloguing in Publication

De Bosset, Farideh, 1945-
        A tilt : poems / Farideh de Bosset.

(Inanna poetry and fiction series)
Also issued in electronic format.
ISBN 978-1-926708-66-9

        I. Title. II. Series: Inanna poetry and fiction series

PS8607.E222T54 2012   C811'.6   C2012-901253-X

Printed and bound in Canada

Inanna Publications and Education Inc.
210 Founders College, York University
4700 Keele Street
Toronto, Ontario, Canada M3J 1P3
Telephone: (416) 736-5356 Fax (416) 736-5765
Email: inanna.publicatons@inanna.ca Website: www.inanna.ca

to you

Contents

A Tilt I

You judge my words
like Carthage God, Baal.
Harsh and unforgiving.
You fear the fertile womb,
the new moon,
the first spring storm.
You fear the fresh breath
erasing the old.

A Tilt II

It was only a thorn
embedded in the flesh of a finger,
confident in its lodging, nesting.
But the flesh raged
against the uninvited guest
protesting and defending
its boundaries. A fight
that only blood
could wash clean.

A Tilt III

The tree sheltered
the crow. Now
darkness belonged
to both. They had
to share it, they
had no choice
somehow they found
common joy
waiting for the sunrise.

A Tilt IV

The dizzying swing
of the rocking chair
comforting.
The tilt menacing enough
to remind of the bitterness
of loss
yet of the sweetness
of not falling.

A Tilt V

They met in a washroom
intermission
of "Oh happy days,"
almost shivering
in their shrivelled skin,
sad and struck by the play,
two strangers sharing
an experience
talking of their lives
spent shovelling paper and laundry,
keeping busy
pleasing the world
with little delight,
sustained by faint hope.
Here they were at the end
of a road and its detritus
seeing their lives played
on the stage. And
then they went back
for the second act.

My Father

When he was not working
enticing women,
squabbling with his wife,
scolding his children,

he recited poetry,
eyes sparkling.
Words too abstract for a child
were lullabies
morphing the house
into a haven for a while.

Poetry
a family heirloom,
a fortress,
mangled and rescued us
but mostly connected us
to life and each other.

On his death bed
verses reinstated his last breath,
a glorious goodbye
and a heavenly legacy.

The First Love I

The teddy bear
you once loved
held tight
in moments of distress
the frayed blanket
you dragged around

You still cherish
in your favourite music,
poems, objects
even religion

Are part you
part the other,
your first love,
often the mother.

The First Love II

I know you.
You belong to the land
of toys and memory.

You are other,
not me,
not you,
yet both,
the world.

Through you
I know I am a girl
who likes to show off her pink skirt.

Through you
I have heard
the Celeste songs
birds chirping in melancholy.

Through you I know sweetness
of taste
immoderately short-lived,
that "forever"
we carry in our souls and cells.

The First Love III

I have loved you
since I met you,
first person in my life.

We danced in many toylands
and candy shops.

Then you were gone.

Years later you came back
in a "grown-up's" train
to take me over continents
and across time.

Now and then you reappear
in ones I love,
in a smell or touch
carrying me
into lightness
that only the breeze
has known.

Working Mother

While you are eating,
peeing
smiling
and playing
I know you are waiting
for one person, your mother.

The hours of the day
pass slowly, slowly.
The sun sets,
you eat supper,
play more
and finally she arrives.

You are both exhausted.
You hardly can smile
at each other now
"No lover's quarrels,"*
just resignation –
child and working mother.

*"I had a lover's quarrel with the world."—Robert Frost's epitaph

My Children

My children are older
my leash is longer.

Their feverish eyes do not raise
so often to stab my heart.

Their demands
may rest for awhile.

My nights are less disturbed.
I am gathering strength
dreaming of tomorrow.

The Summer of Fourteen

Shyly, she walked into the room
She was fourteen,
pimply-faced and chubby,
not a woman, or a child.

Somehow not that lovable
in her awkwardness
until a memory of the summer
I was fourteen, flooded my being.

A summer difficult and confusing
I never left my bed.

A Mother's Fate

My grown-up daughter
it is your time now
to tell me where I've gone wrong.

It is a mother's fate
to lose godly power
bestowed on her
by her child.

Then her humanness
is an outrage
and she is redundant.

She might even be crowned
as Queen of the Night
a danger
to the kingdom
of the self:
Independence.

An Aging Mother

They say you look like me.
Your black eyes
and smile.

A woman,
my daughter in ripe age.
I watch you with delight
wonder how less and less

I look like myself.

Loss

Through life
friends are lost to death,
madness, relocation
but mostly through
the shades of grey
that are coping and change.

Defining the Self

Creators we are
in recreating the lives we've lived
fiction
and canvases
where events are splashed
taking on a new form

by borrowing,
imitating,
deleting and adding
inventing and reinventing
memories and stories
defining the self.

Moments

naked and fresh
never lie.

But dressed up
in the mask of logic, affect
and calendar, adding
up to become hours, days,
years
or a memory...

They lose their identity,
then we will never know
what they were.

The Present

is ephemeral, an elusive
moment,
enveloped by amnesia
of undesirable memories
the denial
of "what is to come".

A glass, full
overflowing
into the unknown.

Everydayness

is a warm blanket
on a chilly day.

The routine soothes,
imitating timelessness,

fooling us into forgetting.

Our Songs

Have we forgotten
our songs
the way crows
by the busy highways;
cackle
only to get by?

A Date

I have a date tonight,
a few hours to kill,
to keep "busy,"

Killing a chunk of my life
waiting.

Alone

Living alone
no dog to kick
no partner to blame –
living without a mirror
having to assume
one's own hell.

Incest

I kissed his forehead
then his cheek
descending towards the neck.

The natural place
would have been the lips.

But I had to stop
fearing the taboo
of incest.

The fortress protecting the purity
of the embrace
in the highest order of spirit,
head and heart
above the nose,
above the lips,
the permissible spheres.

The Breath

My cat knows paradise,
in a ray of sun
where he lies purring,
oblivious
to the storms and chatters
of the world
enjoying breath,
just breath,
divine.

Rosie's Eyes

Rosie had become a pair of eyes,
screaming I am Rosie,
the same girl I was twenty years ago.

The promising star,
now thicker and shorter
make-up and jewellery
covering most of her.

Her dimmer eyes
washed out of dreams
the faint reminder –
what could have been.

Long-Term Marriage

A world
of habitual chores
and groans
with occasional
endearing words.

The rage
of unmet wishes and desires
and many compromises
of lives intermingled.

Now decay
lingers in the air
like the musty stench
of a wound.

Well-bandaged
by a manicured lawn,
a well-kept house
and the shiny brouhaha
of Sunday family do's.

A November Child

They say when it happened
the sky was grey,
the colour of milk,
well skimmed,
pale, blue, thin,
bloodless
and tasteless.
It was a November sky,
useless for summer,
useless for winter.
It had a quality
of lazy middle years,
menopausal,
unfertile,
not fully done.

They say it was drizzling,
not yet raining clearly.

It was November.
The month of your birth,
so in between
so confusing, so you
the child of November and its sky.

November

Month of satiety,
low expectation,
summer consumed,
the land's bounty harvested.

The world is resting
before winter's battle.

The land and sky
unburdened
as free from duty
as swirling leaves.

A ray of sun
or a balmy day
are stolen goods
from gods and goblins
with a mischievous gratitude.

A Peach Tree

He was old and shrivelled
pushing a walker
and buying a peach tree
in a nursery,
discounted at summer's end.

Full of anticipation
at harvesting its juicy fruits.

The Grass

Each blade
tells a story
of months lived underground

dreaming of light
of a caressing breeze
to spring up and dance.

Unaware of the mower's blade
saluting its rise.

Ants

Ants labour for days
to open a peony's bud.
Then are discarded
as pests.

Dormant Lilacs

It is snowing,
the lilacs far away
dormant in their beds,
dreaming of bursting
into colour

Whispering to whoever will listen;
let us be cosy, tucked in longer,
safe from the glory of summer,
the rising demands
for shinier foliage and blossoms
a life span
too short for lovers.

The Sameness

Listen to your friend
talking of her husband
their children,
trials and losses
moments of joy.

Listen to your voices,
not different,
yet with a different tone.

Listen to the waiter,
ready to end his night,
grumpy under a fixed smile.

Listen to the monotony of destinies,
the sameness under the cacophony
of this and that,
the noises of boredom
shut up by action

Then nothing.
Another evening,
a merciful sleep
even dreams.

Hoarding

Tune in to the annihilation of your desires and time.
You accumulate love, passion, maybe knowledge and
hoping...
Hoarding things as if they were your life

Soon love dusts away
like the rotten wing of a butterfly,
leaving a powdery stain
on the tips of your fingers.
Youth follows love,
knowledge rarely turns to wisdom.

Then you hold on to the walls, furniture, clothes, a few
scraps of metal,
stones, piles of papers and books.
Things... Solid things. The remains,
the waste...
And the tick-tock of the clock.
For now.

A Present

is at best a treaty of annexation,
an offering to appease,
or to impress.
at worst it is a blood price.

A well-wrapped box
is a make-believe,
a shell of empty promises,
a rite to enslave,
or to blend into someone else's life.

Poverty

Listen to poverty
soft, timid,
apologetic, appearing
out of a long dark tunnel
of dust and debris.

Smell the acrid, douceâtre,
scent of decay,
neglect and loss.

Tune to the poverty
within, the emptiness,
aching boredom
resignation.

Envy

Tune into that rage,
envy,
the evil-eye,
power of destruction

Listen to yourself,
it may be lurking in you,
inciting you to act, to go to war,
to bite and get your loot.

Listen well,
it may already be doing its job.

The First Quarter of the Moon

When you visit me tonight
I will be bubbly and light.
I will take you to the backyard
to show you the first quarter
of the moon
as big as the tip of your fingernail
shining above the Norwegian pine.
Just as the sun is setting
and sparrows are stirring.

If you dismiss it.
My heart would sink
disconnected and lonely.

Aging

Standing by the pit
made of our lives
where all precious minerals
are removed by the years.

The only nuggets left
are silent moments,
memories
a few poems
to hold
like hot coals
to drop and pick up again
easing the burning pain
of aging.

Doubt

the dreaded
heart-squeezing uncertainty,
glides towards
new lights,
opening the spirit like a fiddlehead
unfurls into the sky.

But certainty
calming and reassuring,
fixed as a hinge on a door
squeaks of dogma.
It limits and shrinks
the air into a bottle.

Youth

We spend our lives
half-drunk with youth,
hope
and what
we think is love.

Finding sobriety
too harsh.
If we're lucky, we will die drunk.

Old Age

an attack of locusts
sudden and devastating
leaving behind
nothing but a barren expanse.

Being Alive

I met life a couple of hours ago.
in a woman dying,
but very alive,
sipping a glass of wine,
telling stories
in the euphoria and calm of morphine,
upright and proud
and stronger than life and death,
knowing the magic and myth
of both.
All her monsters gone
save for the final one,
no longer intimidating

The Ring

The music thunders,
galloping,
singing of power and conquest,
vibrating the house,
shaking the windows
and my back.

Diva

The audience applauded
the Diva
after each aria,
admiring
her beauty,
her voice
her fame.

She sang
"fate" "fate"
hers and theirs,
"faith" "faith"
in life and in the moment

The flame soared
as they applauded the Diva
and themselves.

The Land

The land is brand new to me,
unknown to my ancestors.
It is not my birthplace.

But it has made me its own
as much as herons, muskrats
and frogs in the lake.
We are all pilgrims
hearing each other's prayers
and gratitude.

The land claimed me
as one of its pine and maple
trees.
It found me
hearing my yearning to belong,
less audible
than the chorus
of the Canadian Geese,
always on the go,
agitated,
looking for another settlement,
farther and less visible
than the patches

of the blue sky reappearing
among the cumulus

The geese will fly high to catch
their dreams
leaving me
in the great stretch of the moment
sheltered for now
from the protests of difference
and belonging.

The Accent

The accent is the cadence
of syllables in the voice
like a blemish or a wart,
a birthmark,
acquired through life.
Or, inherited
like an heirloom
to wear
or bear
like a second skin.

A Dreamer

She tickles my heart in her restraint
and abandon. Her hands move
and make shadows so ghost-like,
they are gentle wings
an image in my memory.

I follow with my eyes
a surge of desire
to hold them tight,
then to hold her body,
framed in my heart.

I have a few of her already
etched deep inside.(For rainy days).

I watch the gentleness of those hands.

The Future

And the soil cracked
and the trees tired of waiting
shed their leaves,
the sky blue,
cloudless, pitiless and undisturbed.

The prayers for rain
blown away by dust.

Only one spring continued to run,
determined, consoling.
Life itself, hope,
the promise of future.

It rained,
washing away the dust.

Fear of another drought
spoiled the present,
made it already the past.

A Rainy Year

It was a rainy summer,
the year I met you,
the year of fireflies.

It was the year of dizziness
and dancing.

While the farmers
complained of crops rotting.

It was the year I discovered
losing hope was a sin.

So I prayed for the sun
and foolishly for the miracle
of everlasting love.

The raindrops sang with me.

Insomnia

is a bird
whose wings
have been clipped.
It tries to fly
only to fall on
its impotent body,
frustrated and helpless
waiting to be rescued by dawn.

A Sleepless Night

Another night
of hugging pillows
and aching body,
all alone.

The rain knocking
all night at the window,
mingling with the weeping willow.

I count the raindrops,
trying not to think of you.

The memory of your touch lost
keeps dancing on my wet eyelashes
and the weeping branches of the willow.

The Future Never Came

She hoped and built,
graduated, got awards,
married and had kids.

Loved and popular,
she worked hard and achieved much.

But the future never came,
having lost its way
in the brackish waters
of a busy life
and its promises.

A Love Affair

Northern lights are flirtation
between Heaven and Earth
in their magnetic love.

A bouquet of colourful lights
exchanged in their embrace,
pulsating
with the gratitude
of each having the other.

Secrets

Family secrets shame
spread like a veil,
invisible and dark.

A giant spider web
holding tight.

Waiting

The waiting that is life,

for the magic destination
when portals open
to the sublime

To reach it only
in fleeting moments
when thirsty lips are sated
or arms reached out and held.

Renewal

Each day's event,
every moment
a breeze in the leaves
and raindrops.

Every time
a hand is held
one reached for
and a fist opened
a lip kissed.

A door slammed shut,
another-opened.

The heart changes its beat
and cells their codes
we are different
from the day before.

A Family Gem

It was a piece of wine-coloured stone,
a precious ruby
brought back from a conquest.
Cherished for generations
making everyone proud.
It was a wealth,
glory,
a family crest.

In a reversal of fortune,
everything was gone
except for the stone,
which would keep the family afloat.

It was found
to be as ephemeral
as the rest,
a worthless piece of crystal
and another tale of pride.

Laughter

The world's leaders meet
to dust off the ruins of the market
and stop the bleeding
of despair

In the midst of the arrogance
exhilaration of the power
laughter is heard,
mixed with tears,
sadness of a clown
colourful acts and attire.

Far away,
another roaring is audible
on the horizon
engorged with storm clouds and birds songs.
God laughing
in the rain,
awakened
by the irony

The trees
resigned to the direction of the wind
watching in silence.

Jerusalem

Jerusalem, promised land
reached
from the Mount of Olives

You look so thirsty,
yet somehow sated
by Man's hope
longing to be freed by you
from his earthly restraints

And here you are in your glory
harmonious in your sandy white stones,
bejewelled by the golden crown
of your Dome.

So proud, Jerusalem the peacock,
the eternal merchant of faith,
seducing the flocks
who soon are betrayed
by their belief in Paradise.

But you keep on inviting hope
before turning it dust and blood
to build more limestone temples,

again crumbled by other lovers
of your charm.

Jerusalem the sublime
yet as earthly as Man
who tries to reach God.

The powerful witch,
the vassal of dogma
and broken hearts

Rise,
rise to forgiveness.
Free up Man to look for God
not within your walls
but in the heart.

A Religion

She fasted
like a faithful attending
Matins and Vespers,
every day piously

She prayed
each rosary bead replacing
a well-measured bit of food

She prayed
as God remained silent,
the fat immutable

She prayed
kept on believing
despite the moments of doubt

She rebelled in despair
by changing the rituals

But she held on to her religion
Tight

Flaming Booze

You work not to earn a living
but a life. Worthless
in a land where your measure
is your net worth
and your marriage worth half that

And friendship, a date set
weeks ahead.

A life you end up drinking
like flaming booze.
"Et tu bois cet alcool brûlant
comme ta vie,
ta vie que tu bois comme une eau-de-vie."*

*from "Zone" by Guillaume Apollinaire (*Alcools,* Gallimard, 1913)

A Resurrection

The day before Easter Sunday
a clamour began
within a downpipe
on the side of the house.

A life was struggling
to free itself,
scratching the metal,
climbing up and falling down
again and again.

I went away to forget it
pretending it was solved.
But I could not,
knowing well the feeling
of being trapped
and rotting slowly;
every being's destiny.

This bird in the downpipe
was going to die, tortuously and slowly.

Now I had to act
and found a pair of pliers in the garage

and with some hardship
opened the pipe – a botched job

but made an opening big enough
for the bird, a starling,
young and vigorous
to escape.

Flying fast away,
over the top of the pine trees.

The resurrection of a bird
and of my soul
which flew with the bird
for a moment at least.

A Tree

Africans say that when the sun rises
both gazelle and lion
have to run
I say let me be neither
prey nor predator.

Let me be an acacia tree,
sitting tight,
my branches shelter
against the sun and rain

My leaves rustling gently
inviting birds
to live
and nest.

Cycle of Life

Not unlike salmon
swimming upstream
to the site of their conception
and death,
we continue on a path,
blindly determined
rationalizing the pain,
lured by small pleasures.

Indian Summer

is the flirtation
of a dying man,
a decaying body's final attempt
to rise
and feast once more
on the passion of youth.

Death

I know you,
met you
in a moment of loss,
in treason
and in long nights of silence.

You are in your glory
in the bitterness of hate
and war
So in the final moments
as you take my breath way,
I salute you

Farewell

Leaning on her walker
she stepped out of bed
to the window
looking at snow falling
(white as her hair)
and snow-covered trees.

Eyes laden with nostalgia
saying farewell:
I will not see you again
until I am part of you

Acknowledgements

Every time I speak of my poetry, I am asked if I write in Farsi, French or English. These are the three languages of my daily life. But I have been living, teaching and working in an English speaking country for over forty years. Daily, I read, write and speak in English, albeit with an accent. How could I write in any other language but English?

When I told my mother that I was writing poetry in English, she was silent for a moment. Then she said, "Poetry? What poetry? All poetry has already been written thousands of years ago in Farsi. There is nothing new to say, especially in a second language."

My parents fostered in me a deep love of poetry. As a child and teenager, before I left Iran for Switzerland to begin my medical studies at the age of eighteen, poetry was the language of our household; that was the way my parents communicated with each other, and with me. At the time, I thought poetry too ethereal and that only through science I could truly understand human nature. Later I realized that science and literature or poetry were actually complementary in grasping the mystery of human nature and life.

Somehow, we end up where we are, doing with what we have, living on "a tilt" most of the time, but finding our path as it is laid out before us.

I have always been fortunate to come across people who have been saviours of others, recognizing the potential in other people and in me. As a result I have had devoted and extraordinary mentors such as Luciana Ricciutelli, Vicky Drummond, and an anonymous editor who helped me to grow, even in my advanced age. Others who helped me along the way are Julia Kuzeljevich, Debbie Wright, Rina Berardi, my wonderful muse, Tressa Fox, and my dear family: my husband Philippe and my children Vanessa, Christopher, Costanza and especially my son, Aurele, my tireless cheerleader. I feel blessed and am forever grateful to all of them.

This first collection of my poems is dedicated to my muses — every person I meet every day: my friends, family members, my students and my patients, with my deepest gratitude.

Some of these poems have previously appeared, often in earlier versions, in the following publications: *Canadian Woman Studies/ les cahiers de la femme*; *Carousel*; and *Other Tongues: Mixed-Race Women Speak Out* (Inanna Publications 2009).

Photo: Al Gilbert C. M.

Farideh de Bosset was born in Tehran, Iran, where poetry is part of everyday life and conversation. At the age of 18, she moved to Switzerland to study medicine. She obtained her medical degree in 1971. She interned in Quebec and then moved to Toronto in 1972 for her residency. She received her fellowship in Psychiatry in 1976, and was a staff psychiatrist and assistant professor in psychiatry at the University of Toronto until 1991, when she established her private practice. Her poetry has been published in a number of literary journals across Canada. She lives and writes in Toronto. Visit her website at <www.FaridehdeBosset.ca>.